T0323581

MANAGING THE
FINANCES OF A FAMILY

MOTHOFELA R. MSIMANGA, PhD

MANAGING THE FINANCES OF A FAMILY

by

MOTHOFELA R. MSIMANGA

Published by Bhiyoza Publishers (Pty) Ltd

First edition, first impression 2020
ISBN: 978-0-620-89865-2 – Managing the Family Finances

Cover credits:

Main image: supplied by author

vectore images: vectorstock (Image #751791 at VectorStock.com) (Image #2540085 at VectorStock.com)

Disclaimer: *Managing the Finances of a Family* is not financial advice, but it is a book in which the author offers his views on how the finances of a family can be managed properly to achieve financial sustainability. This book should not be regarded as financial advice; readers should consult their financial advisors when they need financial advice.

DEDICATION

This book is dedicated to my late mother, Elina Mametsing Msimanga who succumbed to Coronavirus in August 2020. This book is the blessing to the fruit of her womb.

PREFACE AND ACKNOWLEDGEMENTS

Managing the Finances of a Family is a book that aims to help its readers to achieve financial sustainability. Many books focus on how people can get rich but, in this book, the author acknowledges that no one can get rich if the person is striving for survival. Therefore, the book focuses on how families and family members can achieve financial sustainability. The contents of the book are aimed at the lower middle class and the working class. The reader should remember that the book is more relevant to the lower middle class and the working class as the book is contextualised to address how they can manage their finances, but the book can be useful to other classes of society.

The book is structured in a manner that allows the reader to understand a concept before the application of the concept is demonstrated. This book touches on a subject that many people usually try to avoid and because of that, they end by giving up on their journey to financial sustainability. The book allows the reader to do an introspection on personal and/or family finances to develop a plan to achieve financial sustainability. Since the book is not a sponsored book nor a marketing campaign book, it addresses issues without benefitting any organisation; instead, it is meant to benefit the reader. If the readers can follow and implement the suggestions in this book, they can improve on how they manage their finances. Noteworthy, is that the contents of this book are not imaginary but are based on practical application.

I would like to express my gratitude to Free State Baptist Men's Department and Eastern Free State Baptist Men's Department for affording me the opportunity to share my views about managing the finances during their rallies. The feedback that I received after my presentations encouraged me to write this book and share my views with a broader community.

I must express my appreciation to my wife Nonhlanhla Msimanga, for allowing me to use our time to write this book and above all for allowing me to use our experiences in the book.

Mothofela R. Msimanga (PhD)
2020

TABLE OF CONTENTS

No.	Contents	Page No.

CHAPTER 3
FAMILY FINANCIAL PLANNING

CHAPTER 4
FAMILY BUDGETING

CHAPTER 5
FAMILY FINANCIAL PROCESSES:- ORGANISATION, IMPLEMENTATION AND CONTROL

CHAPTER 6
THE CAUSES OF FINANCIAL PROBLEMS IN FAMILIES AND DEALING WITH IDENTIFIED PROBLEMS

CHAPTER 7
PRACTICAL WAYS OF SAVING SOME MONEY

CHAPTER 8
UNDERSTANDING ISSUES WHICH HAVE FINANCIAL IMPACT ON MIDDLE CLASS, LOW CLASS AND THE UNEMPLOYED

Page left intentionally blank

CHAPTER

1

ADMINISTRATION OF FINANCIAL ACTIVITIES OF A FAMILY

1.1   Introduction

'A family' refers to parents living with their children; a group of people who are related in any other way; a group of people who share the same bloodline or a group of people who live together in the same household. This book adopts the latter definition of a family: "a group of people who live in the same household". When a group of people belong to the same household, they form an organisation, because an organisation is formed by a structured social unit of people who have the same goals in being together. A family meet this criterion for defining an organisation because in a family there are people living and spending time together. Therefore, since a family is an organisation, it should have rules that guide its activities. The focus of this chapter is on the administration of the financial activities of a family. Family financial activities in the context of this book refer to all the actions which affect the monies of a family. To administer the financial activities of a family, families should have structures put in place. These structures, amongst others, include: setting the rules for managing family finances, provision of financial leadership, discussions about the finances of the family, taking financial responsibility, financial accountability and the importance financial contribution by all family members who have a source of income. There next section discusses the rules for managing family finances.

1.2   The rules for managing family finances

For a family to be well organised and well managed, it should set out rules which guide the conduct of its members. Organisations such as churches, political parties and work environments all have rules that guide them. Even families have rules concerning how to live. Families have rules for how members of the family should behave in the family. There are rules about households' chores such cleaning the house, washing dishes, cooking, and cleaning the gardens. There are also general rules about the time when children should be at home, how they should behave at home and in public, religion, good health, and relationships. But many families do not have rules on how to deal with the finances.

Owing to this absence of rules on managing the finances of the family, family members spent money randomly. In some families every member of the family buys what he/she wants to buy when they like and at times there is duplication of products purchased. One family member might spend his/her money on things that do not benefit the family, but the family member benefits from the money spent by other family members. Families can manage their finances appropriately if they set rules that guide how to manage those finances. The rules on managing family finances can include, amongst others: family financial plans, meetings on financial matters and contributions by family members. The implementation of rules needs someone from the family who can take leadership on enforcement of the rules.

1.3   Leadership on family financial activities

Parents, by virtue of their status in the family, are expected to give leadership on family matters. In many families, the father is regarded as the head or leader of the family but there are many families which are led by mothers even when the father is available. The leadership role in different families depends on the qualities that each parent possesses. Leadership qualities are more important in leading the family rather than who is the father or the mother. The same applies regarding the leadership in relation to the family's finances.

Family members should not lead the finances of the family by virtue of their status in the family; rather, this role should be filled by someone who has a talent for financial management. Any member of the family can provide leadership in managing family's finances as long as the family member is skilled in financial management. In some families, the father is the one who manages the finances; in most families, the mother is the one who manages the finances and in other families, one of the children manages the finances. The reasons for the variation on who manages the finances in each family are different but there are three common qualities the families look into when deciding on who should manage the family's finances. When a family chooses a family member who will take financial leadership in the matter of the family finances, they do not look into who contributes more than other family members but instead they look for a family member who is able to communicate, who shows responsibility and who is prepared to account in his/her role.

1.4   Communication about family finances

Families discuss different aspects of life which affect them. They discuss issues around education, politics, religion, and events that took place, amongst others. Many families fail to have discussions around family finances, and therefore I say this is one of the issues which needs someone to lead the process. A family member who should deal with family finances should be a good communicator. He/she should be able to relate well with all other members of the family. The person should be able to approach those who do not follow the set rules on finances and update other family members about any financial discrepancies in the family. Communication about family finances can be formal or informal. Communication skills are very important because if reported issues cannot be communicated appropriately, a family can have a serious fight. Family meetings should be organised where the finances of the family are discussed, and it is the responsibility of a person who leads the finances of the family to arrange such meetings.

1.5   Family finances responsibility

The person who manages the finances of the family should be a person who is responsible. This family member who manages the finances of the family is responsible for enforcing the rules that have been agreed upon. The first sign of responsibility regarding the family finances is contributing the agreed upon amount on/or before the agreed date and compliance with all the rules relating to family finances. Another form of responsibility is to ensure that all members of the family who should contribute do contribute the agreed amount on/or before the agreed date. The money received should be spent on items agreed upon and family financial plans consulted before family money is spent.

1.6   Family finances accountability

The person who manages the finances of the family should keep the financial records of the family, such as financial plans, amounts received, and payments made. Family members, including young children who are not contributing, should be given reports on regular basis to ensure that every family member is on board on the financial status of the family. The reports should cover all the financial activities of the family. Monies that are unaccounted for might create problems in the family; thus, it is important for family finances to be managed by a person who can account without having problems about being accountable. When there are regular updates on family finances, family members will work together to ensure that there is financial stability in the family. Furthermore, the person who leads the family finances should know that he/she will be accountable for any irregularities regarding the financial matters of the family. Based on this, it is evident that accountability brings family members closer to each other, as it is important for family members to work together to ensure that family finances are well managed.

1.7   Family members working together and family finances

Composition of families differs in terms of who makes up the family and the number of family members. Some families comprise a couple where only two people live together. Some families comprise a couple and their children. Some families consist of a single parent and one or many children. Some families consist of children only. Some of the children in the families are young, others are old and some of the children already have a source of income. Some families are made up of relatives living together. In other families, there might be extended family members living with the family. The extended family members might have a source of income or not have a source of income. These dynamics of families demonstrate the complexities of managing the family and often make it even more complex to manage the finances of that family.

It is important that family members work together as a family regarding the finances. All family members who have a source of income including children who have a source of income should make a financial contribution for the wellbeing of the family. Family members who have a source of income should not expect to benefit from financial contributions made by other family members while they do not contribute. The more people in the family contribute the lesser the burden on other members because more money will be available for the use by the whole family. The financial wellbeing of the family can be easily improved when all the members of the family work towards the same goal.

1.8   Conclusion

In this introductory chapter of the book, a family as an organisation is discussed and put into context of the book as a group of people who live in the same household. The book's context of family financial activities is explained. Organisations have rules and regulations that regulate them; thus, the need for having rules on managing family finances is discussed. The importance of leadership in family finances is highlighted and the three key qualities of a person who should manage the finances of the family are identified as communication, responsibility, and accountability. Firstly, such a person should possess the necessary communication skills so he/she can speak to different family members and address all issues pertaining to the family's finances. Secondly, he or she has the responsibility of ensuring that money is spent according to the family plans. Thirdly, he or she must demonstrate accountability by reporting on money received and money spent. The importance of family members working together and the importance of all family members who have a source of income to make financial contributions towards the financial wellbeing of the family is highlighted.

The next chapter will focus on the family's Statement of Net Worth. I regard this as the first step towards sustainability in family finances because it can help families to know where they should start when it comes to dealing with their finances.

CHAPTER

2

STATEMENT OF NET WORTH OF THE FAMILY

2.1 Introduction

The previous chapter focused on how to administer the financial activities of a business. This chapter deals with the Statement of Net Worth of a family. A Statement of Net Worth of a family gives an indication about the financial position of the family. To give a better understanding of a financial position of the family, the assets and liabilities of the family should be identified. This chapter focuses on family assets, family liabilities and lastly, the Statement of Net Worth of a family.

2.2 Family assets

Assets are all items which have a lasting monetary value. Family assets can be regarded as all such items which are owned by members of a family individually or collectively. Family assets can be tangible or intangible assets. Tangible assets of a family are also referred to as fixed assets or non-current assets, while intangible assets of a family are also referred to as current assets. In this book the concepts "non-current assets and current assets" are used. Family assets are used to prepare the Statement of Net Worth of the family.

2.2.1 Family non-current assets

Family non-current assets are the assets of a family that are physical and can be seen or touched. These assets cannot be easily converted to cash because they need another person to be involved before they can be converted to cash, such as someone who would be prepared to buy them. Examples of family non-current assets are:

- Residential property such as a house or apartment (not rented)
- Residential sites not yet developed
- Cars, motorbikes, and bicycles
- Equipment such as garden tools, gymnasium equipment, computer equipment, household equipment
- Furniture such as dining room suites, lounge suites and bedroom suites
- Crockery
- Cell phones
- Clothes and shoes
- This list of family non-current assets differs from family to family.

The value of some of the non-current assets appreciates while the value of other non-current assets depreciates, which means the value of some non-current assets increases over time while the value of some non-current assets decreases over time. It is important for families to buy more of non-current assets which appreciate than buying those that depreciate. The logic for this is that when non-current assets appreciate, their value increases and the asset can be sold at a higher price, which is a gain to the family. Buying more non-current assets which depreciate it is a loss over time because the assets would have to be sold at the lower price than their original cost price. The value of residential property normally appreciates but the value of cars depreciates; therefore, families should consider this when buying non-current assets. Noteworthy, is that the value of property normally appreciates in response to supply and demand.

2.2.2 Family current assets

Current assets of a family are the assets that family members own but which are not physical, such as invested money. These assets can be easily converted to cash because what a family member need is just to contact a financial institution to convert the current asset to cash. Examples of family current assets are:

- Cash and cash equivalents such as amounts kept in a bank account
- Investments such as shares, money market investments, unit trusts, fixed deposits, and notice deposits
- Debtors
- Investments in stokvels
- This list of family current assets differs from family to family.

The value of family current assets increases in value due to return on investments. The value of cash at the bank increases slightly due to interest earned if this happens. The value of shares increases or decreases due to the stability in the financial markets and other factors. The value of interest-bearing investments increases based on the rate of interest. The rate of interest can be calculated as simple interest or compound interest. Families should note that investments which earns compound interest receive higher returns than investments which receive simple interest. The reason is that simple interest is calculated on original investment amount while compound interest is calculated on original investment amount and the interest already earned. Compounded interest is beneficial to family members as the return on investment will be higher over the years.

2.3   Family liabilities

Liabilities are monies that are owed to other people or organisations who are creditors. Family liabilities comprise the total amounts that family members owe to other people or organisations. Family liabilities attract interest; therefore, family members should carefully compare deals offered by different credit granters when looking for credit. Some organisations charge higher interest rates and that overburdens family members. Liabilities are classified as non-current liabilities or long-term liabilities and current liabilities or short-term liabilities. In this book the concepts "non-current liabilities and current liabilities" are used. Family liabilities are used to prepare the Statement of Net Worth of the family.

2.3.1 Family non-current liabilities

Family non-current liabilities are the amounts owed by family members to other people or organisations which are repayable over a long period, normally over years. Examples of family non-current liabilities are:

- Loans on property
- Instalment car purchases
- Instalment equipment purchases
- Instalment furniture purchases
- Long-term loans
- Credit cards
- Study loans
- This list of family non-current liabilities differs from family to family.

Families spend a great deal of income on financing non-current liabilities repayment and paying interest on non-current liabilities. Families should note that the amount they pay as an instalment slightly reduces the principal debt because interest is added monthly. Family members should add up monthly interest paid to non-current liabilities; they will be surprised to see how much they lose every month.

2.3.2 Family current liabilities

Family current liabilities are amounts owed by the family members to other people or organisations, which amounts are repayable within a short period of time, usually less than a year. Examples of family non-current liabilities are:

- Short-term loans
- Store credit cards
- Short-term credit purchases
- Bank overdrafts
- Creditors
- This list of family current liabilities differs from family to family.

Family current liabilities such as store credit cards do not attract interest when purchases are made and paid for over six months. This is one of the benefits family members should exploit. Family current liabilities are charged higher interest rates because they are unsecured and regarded as risky. Some lenders charge more than the maximum set interest rate. Most family members, when they cannot pass an affordability test (credit check) at financial institutions, resort to other organisations who are not regulated in microfinancing and then end up being exploited. Family members end up relying on these unregulated micro-lenders and end up working to repay a recurring debt. When family members repay the amount owed, they take another loan and they get deeper into the debt trap. A strategy should be developed on how family members can get out of any debt traps they might be in.

2.4   Statement of Net Worth of a family

The Statement of Net Worth of a family is the statement that indicates whether a family is solvent or bankrupt. It is the statement that indicates the net worth of the family or the financial position of the family. If the value of family assets is higher than the value of family liabilities, the family is solvent but if the value of family assets is lower than the value of family liabilities, the family is bankrupt. If the Statement of Net Worth of a family shows a positive (+) balance that means the family is solvent while a negative (-) balance will mean that the family is bankrupt.

It is important for families to be solvent which indicates that a family can meet its obligations. When families are solvent, they can easily access credit from financial institutions, and they can bargain for lower interest rates. It is important for families to use their solvency status for their financial benefit. Families that are bankrupt do not easily get access to credit at regulated institutions and end up approaching unregulated lenders who in many instances exploit them, as detailed above. A Statement of Net Worth can be used as a point of departure towards the financial stability of the family. It can be used to determine how a family can plan for future actions involving finances.

2.4.1 Assets in the Statement of Net Worth of a family

All assets owned by family members are added together using their current value. Assets which appreciate will have a higher value compared to the original purchase value and assets which depreciate will have a lower value compared to the original purchase price. The value of property might be higher than the original value of purchase, while the value of a car will be lower than the original purchase value.

2.4.2 Liabilities in the Statement of Net Worth of a family

All liabilities of family members are added together using the current balance owed. The amount owed for some liabilities will be higher than the original debt even when the payments have been made. The reason for this is that interest is already calculated and added for the whole amount during of the liability term. In other instances, the amount owed will be slightly lower than the original debt when payments have been made. The reason for this is that the interest charged is higher in initial years of the liability because it is charged on a higher balance.

2.5 Preparing a Statement of Net Worth of a family

The Statement of Net Worth of a family is prepared by adding up all the assets to get their total value and adding up all the liabilities to determine the total amount owed. The total amount owed is subtracted from the total value of assets. The difference is used to determine solvency or bankruptcy as discussed in section 2.4 above.
Below are different approaches of how to prepare a Statement of Net Worth of a family.

The following information of Hlubi family is available to prepare the Statement of Net Worth of this family as at 30 June 2020:

House	R 300 000.00
Car	R 90 000.00

Furniture	R 80 000.00
Garden tools	R 3 000.00
Household equipment	R 10 000.00
Computer equipment	R 7 000.00
Music system	R 4 000.00
Fixed deposit	R 45 000.00
Bank balance	R 12 000.00
Unit trusts	R 20 000.00
Crockery	R 8 000.00
Cell phones	R 12 000.00
Clothes and shoes	R 20 000.00
Car balance	R 30 000.00
Long term-loans	R120 000.00
Furniture stores balance	R 40 000.00
Credit cards	R 35 000.00
Clothing stores balances	R 3 000.00
Personal loans	R 15 000.00
Creditors	R 7 000. 00

Horizontal approach
Statement of Net Worth of Hlubi family as at 30 June 2020

Assets			Liabilities		
House	300 000	00	Car balance	30 000	00
Car	90 000	00	Long-term loans	120 000	00
Furniture	80 000	00	Furniture stores	40 000	00
Garden tools	3 000	00	Credit cards	35 000	00
Household equipment	10 000	00	Clothing stores balance	3 000	00
Computer equipment	7 000	00	Personal loans	15 000	00
Music system	4 000	00	Creditors	7 000	00
Fixed deposit	45 000	00			
Bank balance	12 000	00			
Unit trusts	20 000	00			
Crockery	8 000	00			

cont.

Cell phones	12 000	00			
Clothes and shoes	20 000	00			
Total assets	**611 000**	**00**	**Total liabilities**	**250 000**	**00**
Net worth				**361 000**	**00**

Vertical approach

Statement of Net Worth of Hlubi family as at 30 June 2020

Assets			**611 000**	**00**
House	300 000	00		
Car	90 000	00		
Furniture	80 000	00		
Garden tools	3 000	00		
Household equipment	10 000	00		
Computer equipment	7 000	00		
Music system	4 000	00		
Fixed deposit	45 000	00		
Bank balance	12 000	00		
Unit trusts	20 000	00		
Crockery	8 000	00		
Cell phones	12 000	00		
Clothes and shoes	20 000	00		
Liabilities			**250 000**	**00**
Car balance	30 000	00		
Long-term loans	120 000	00		
Furniture stores	40 000	00		
Credit cards	35 000	00		
Clothing stores balance	3 000	00		
Personal loans	15 000	00		
Creditors	7 000	00		
Net worth			**361 000**	**00**

Vertical approach using a single column

Statement of Net Worth of Hlubi family as at 30 June 2020

Assets	611 000	00
House	300 000	00
Car	90 000	00
Furniture	80 000	00
Garden tools	3 000	00
Household equipment	10 000	00
Computer equipment	7 000	00
Music system	4 000	00
Fixed deposit	45 000	00
Bank balance	12 000	00
Unit trusts	20 000	00
Crockery	8 000	00
Cell phones	12 000	00
Clothes and shoes	20 000	00
Liabilities	**250 000**	**00**
Car balance	30 000	00
Long-term loans	120 000	00
Furniture stores	40 000	00
Credit cards	35 000	00
Clothing stores balance	3 000	00
Personal loans	15 000	00
Creditors	7 000	00
Net worth	**361 000**	**00**

(Approaches adapted from Msimanga, 2016)

The Statement of Net Worth of Hlubi family as at 30 June 2020 shows that total assets amounted to R 611 000.00 and total liabilities amounted to R 250 000.00 which translates to a net worth of R 361 000.00 because of a positive balance. This family is solvent, but it can increase its solvency by taking certain actions. The family can use some of its investments to pay off some of its debts because the interest earned on investment is normally lower than the interest paid on liabilities. The family can use its cash in the bank to pay off its creditors because there is very low interest (if any is paid) that is earned on bank balance than the interest charged by the creditors if they charge interest (which they usually do). This statement gives a family a clue on which debts can be paid off first if additional money is available. There are a number of financial actions that a family can take to improve their solvency, but this will depend on what the Statement of Net Worth looks like.

2.6   Conclusion

This chapter introduced the Statement of Net Worth of a family. Assets and liabilities were discussed as key components of preparing the Statement of Net Worth. The implications of assets and liabilities on the net worth of a family were discussed. A Statement of Net Worth of a family was presented and interpreted. The chapter highlighted the importance of net worth to the families and showed that the Statement of Net Worth is a point of departure for financial planning. Having determined how the family can gauge its financial position, the next chapter discusses financial planning.

CHAPTER

3

FAMILY FINANCIAL PLANNING

3.1 Introduction

The previous chapter focused on determining the net worth of a family which in turn is used to determine whether a family is solvent or bankrupt. The results of the Statement of Net Worth are used to make financial plans of a family. This chapter focuses on financial plans of a family. Short-term financial planning, medium-term financial planning and long-term financial planning of a family are discussed. The last section of this chapter discusses debt management plans.

Many family members earn income and spend money without considering how their current expenditure will impact their financial stability. It is important for families to have long-term, medium-term and short-term financial plans. Planning is one of the management tasks th involves identifying future activities which must be performed to achieve set objectives. Therefore, family financial planning involves identifying activities which must be undertaken by family members to achieve financial stability. The Statement of Net Worth of a family can be used to identify the financial status of the family and that provide a guide on what must be done to achieve a set goal (financial stability). Family financial planning should meet the criteria of being specific, measurable, realistic and time bound. The plan should be clearly stated, indicate expected results, be achievable with available resources within the set time. All members of a family, including children, should participate in developing financial plans of the family, to ensure that every member of the family is focused on the same financial goals.

3.2 Short-term financial planning of a family

Short-term financial planning of a family refers to all financial plans of a family that have a timeframe of less than a year. These financial plans are based on financial goals which can be achieved on a daily, weekly, monthly and annual basis. Families should plan for their daily expenditure such a money for bread, weekly expenditure such as entertainment, monthly expenditure such as rates and taxes and annual expenditure such as birthday celebrations. It is important for family members to plan for these activities because many families spend randomly on short-term expenditure. This is where financial problems start because these expenditures appear minor but when they are added up they take a lot of the family's money.

There are a number of short-term expenditures incurred by family members which cause financial problems, these are just a few of them. Some families do not know who should buy the bread each day, for example and family members end up spending without a plan. At times family members end up fighting over this problem which can be sorted out by financial planning. Some family members spend a lot of money on entertainment without planning first and that leads to overspending. Rates and taxes are not paid, and municipalities are bankrupt because families do not plan how to pay. When families do not have sufficient money this is one of the expenditures they default on. There are families who celebrate birthdays of family members by holding impromptu birthday parties and this creates a gap in the finances which, at times, becomes difficult to close. The preceding discussions demonstrate how easily a family can find itself in financial instability because it did not have a short-term financial planning. Moreover, a number of family fights emanate from these unplanned expenditures. This section should serve as an eye-opener for families about the importance of short-term financial planning. Each family can identify the short-term expenditure which affect its financial stability and start to have short-term financial planning. Short-term financial planning has an impact on medium-term and long-term financial planning because if families struggle to finance short-term expenditure, they will find it difficult to finance medium-term and long-term expenditure.

3.3 Medium-term financial planning of a family

Medium-term financial planning of a family refers to all financial plans of a family that have a timeframe of one to three years. These financial plans are based on financial goals that can be accomplished within three years. Families should plan for buying cell phones, equipment, and furniture. Families that do not have a medium-term financial planning become victim of marketing because they do not know what they want to buy and end up buying what is sold to them. If family members have financial plans, they can resist any marketing persuasion and they will not easily get into debts because they will know what to buy and when to buy.

There are family members who buy whatever is sold to them without looking at their financial status and determining whether they need what is sold or not. Often, a person will have more than one cell phone and will be able to give "good reasons" for having many cell phones. In many instances they give the same reasons which were given to them by the marketers of the cell phones and those reasons are not important to the person who bought the cell phone. The person has more pressing financial issues than seeing that they have many cell phones. Many families have plenty of equipment that they bought but never use. Some of the equipment is not yet paid off and some of it has been used once but their warranties have expired, which is waste of money. Some family members replace their family furniture if they come across something that they like even though the furniture at home is still in good condition. All these cases can be easily avoided if families have medium-term plans which will guide family members on what, when and how they should spend their money.

3.4 Long-term financial planning of a family

Long-term financial planning of a family refers to all financial plans of a family that have a timeframe of more than three years but not indefinite. These financial plans are based on financial goals which can be accomplished over a period of more than three years. Families should plan for buying a car and how to achieve financial stability. Many are the times that people will be worried and say that they want to get out of debt but do nothing to achieve that. Long-term financial planning is one of the ways that can be used to achieve financial stability. Another problem is that people want to quickly get out of debts and end up getting deeper into debts. One of the solutions to getting out of debts is by having a long-term financial plan.

Family members should prepare a long-term financial plan when they want to buy assets like cars. You will meet someone who will proudly tell you how he/she surprised his/her partner with a new family car. If a person buys the car cash and has the money to do that, there is no problem but if that is done on instalment purchase there is a serious problem. A family might be heading towards a financial disaster. Buying a car on instalment purchase involves paying for insurance on top of the monthly instalment and if this is not well calculated the financial problems will start. After looking into the Statement of Net Worth of a family, families should prepare a long-term financial plan which can improve its financial status. A plan should clearly state all the actions which will be taken within set timeframes. Debt-management plans can be used in this regard.

3.5 Debt-management plans

In this book, debt-management plans refer to all activities undertaken to be debt free. Debt-management plans include all actions put into practice to achieve a set goal of being debt free. Families should have a plan to achieve financial stability and one of the things that can facilitate that is getting out of debts. Family members who are debt free spend their money to satisfy their needs and wants rather than spending it on interest and other charges. To validate this statement, family members should add all their monthly interest charges and all charges related to credit they pay every month; some might see that a great deal of hard-earned income is transferred to credit granters. Reducing debts or being debt free is one of the things that can make families to live a normal life. Financial problems in many families lead to serious family problems and that can be avoided by living a debt free life, therefore, debt management is very important.

3.5.1 Approaches to debt management

The first step in approaching debt management is to identify debts that charge higher interest rates, debts with higher instalment and debts with lower balances. People are normally undecided on what to do when they have additional cash at their disposal. In many cases, the available money is often not spent wisely; sometimes, it should be used to pay off the debts. These approaches should be based on family financial plans because it will be a futile exercise to pay off debts and then not know what to do with available cash. Again, it will not be beneficial to pay off one debt and start a new debt later. Debt management is not a once-off activity; it is part of the medium-term to long-term financial plan. Approaching debt management appropriately can result in families being debt free in less than five years but people need to practise patience.

3.5.1.1 Targeting debts with higher interest rate

A person can decide to target debts with higher interest rates with the available cash. The benefit of targeting debts with higher interest rates is that there will be a monthly saving on interest and the saving can be significant over a longer period. The argument for this approach is that it is no use to pay off debts with lower interest rates while you pay more interest on other debts. This can be seen as a loss over a period of time. The benefits of this approach depend on the amount still owed.

3.5.1.2 Targeting debts with higher instalments

A person could decide to target debts with higher instalment. The benefit of targeting a debt with higher instalment is that if that debt is paid off, more money is quickly available to repay other debts. The argument for this approach is that more money becomes available and there are savings on interest and other charges. The instalment saved from this approach can be used to fast-track repayment of other debts; as more debts are paid off, more money will be available to pay off other debts.

3.5.1.3 *Targeting debts lower balances*

A person could decide to pay off debts with lower balances first. The benefit of targeting debts with lower balances is that the instalments amounts paid monthly are reduced and extra cash is available. Extra cash that is available from the instalment that is paid off can be used to increase the amount paid to other debts with lower balances. The argument for this approach is that many debts can be paid off in a short period of time while saving on interest and other charges. The more debts are paid off, the more extra money becomes available and that can be used as additional instalments to other debts.

3.6   Conclusion

In this chapter the importance of family financial planning was emphasised. Short-term financial planning, medium-term financial planning and long-term financial planning of a family were discussed. The importance and the impact of planning for daily, weekly, monthly, annual, one to three years and over three years financial activities were discussed. Lastly, debt management and the approaches to debt management were discussed, while emphasising that new debts should not be created during the debt management period. The next chapter will focus on family budgeting.

CHAPTER
4

FAMILY BUDGETING

4.1 Introduction

The previous chapter dealt with financial plans of a family and the debt-management plans of a family. In this chapter, family budgeting is discussed as a strategy used to implement family financial plans. Family income and family expenditure are discussed in relation to a family budget. Then, a preparation of a family budget is discussed by explaining the steps in preparing a family budget and a family budget is presented. The next section discusses family income.

4.2 Family income

Family income comprises all monies earned by family members from different sources. When preparing a budget, family income is based on all the net incomes of family members. Examples of family income:
- Rent income
- Profit
- Wages/Salaries/Commission
- Interest income

These sources of family income are broad sources of income which can be divided into different categories of income. Family members earn rent income when they own a property that is used by other people; they earn profit when they are involved in business activities, and they earn wages/salaries/commission for their labour. Interest income would be earned as a return on their investments.

When a family budget is drawn, all the income earned by family members is added together. This will differ from family to family depending on how each family manages family finances. Family members might agree to contribute a certain amount of money towards family budget to cater for specific expenditure and the total contribution of each member will be added together. The family will draw its budget based on the total income of the family. Some families might decide to have a joint budget on certain budget items; therefore, total income will be income meant to be spent on identified budget items. In the context of this book, family income is the total income earned by different members of a family.

4.3 Family expenditure

Family expenditure refers to all the expenses incurred by the family on short-term, medium-term, and long-term expenditure. When preparing a budget, family expenditure will not include expenses deducted by stop orders (deductions made directly from income) but will include debit orders (payments deducted from a bank account). Examples of family expenditure:

- Car repayment
- Long-term loans repayment
- Short-term loans repayment
- Furniture repayment
- Credit card repayment
- Debts repayments
- Cell phone
- Education
- Rates and taxes
- Water
- Electricity
- Medical costs
- Clothes and shoes
- Groceries
- Entertainment
- Transport
- Insurance
- Donations paid
- Television subscription
- Security
- Employees' salaries
- Stokvels
- Savings and investments

These are some of the more common expenditures that families can incur but they will differ from family to family. When a family's expenditure is considered, it is important to prioritise expenditure in terms of needs and wants of a family, fixed expenditure of a family and variable expenditure of a family.

4.3.1 Needs and wants of a family

The needs of a family refer to all goods and services which are necessary for the survival of family members while the wants of the family refer to all goods and services which improve the quality of life of family members. There are many debates on these concepts, but this book does not delve into that debate, it just simplifies the concepts for its readers. It is important that when a family budget is prepared the needs should be the first budget items to be allocated amounts. For example, it will not make any sense to allocate money for entertainment, but nothing is allocated for groceries or allocate money for investment, but nothing is allocated for transport to go to work.

4.3.2 Fixed expenditure of a family

Fixed expenditure of a family refers to the expenses of a family which do not vary over a period of time. The allocation of these expenses remains the same over a period of time. They help families to plan knowing the amount to be paid over a certain period of time. Some of the examples are education, insurance, television subscriptions and employees' salaries.

4.3.3 Variable expenditure of a family

Variable expenditure of family refers to expenses of a family that change on monthly basis. They increase during peak periods and decrease during off-peak periods. Management of this expenditure needs thorough planning because they might disturb a family budget as the amounts change regularly. During winter, for example, the cost of electricity will be higher compared to summer. Families should note that the more they buy electricity the higher the rate is that is charged; it would therefore be preferable if they do not reduce the units of electricity they buy in summer to cater for winter. During COVID-19 lockdown families spent more money on groceries because every family member stayed at home, but the money spent on transport was lower because travelling was restricted. Therefore, money saved on transport could be used for augmenting the money spent on groceries. When a family budget is prepared, variable costs should be dealt with in a manner that will be beneficial.

4.4   Preparing a family budget

A family budget is a written document that indicates the expected income of a family and expected expenditure of a family. A family budget is prepared before income is earned and before payments are made. Families should ensure that their income always exceed the expenditure for a family budget to have a surplus. When expenditure exceeds income, a family budget will be in deficit, which must always be avoided. The budget should be updated monthly. It is wiser to prepare monthly family budgets for the whole year because it will be easier to identify and plan for the variations in income and expenditure. There are steps to be followed to prepare a family budget.

4.4.1   Steps in drawing a family budget

The following 8 steps for preparing a family budget are taken from (Msimanga, 2016):

Step 1 – Make a list of all the income to be received
Step 2 – Add up the amounts to get the total income
Step 3 – Make a list of all possible expenditure
Step 4 – Add up the amounts to get the total expenditure
Step 5 – Subtract the total expenditure from the total income
Step 6 – Determine whether there is a deficit or surplus
Step 7 – Review the budget
Step 8 – Rewrite your adjusted budget

4.4.2   A family budget

Different formats of a family budget are presented in this section.
The following information of the Motloung family is available to prepare
a family budget for the month of June 2020:

Rent income	R 7 500.00
Profit	R 4 500.00
Salaries	R 35 000.00
Interest income	R 2 000.00
Car repayment	R 6 500.00
Long-term loans repayment	R 1 800.00
Short-term loans repayment	R 1 200.00
Furniture repayment	R 4 000.00
Credit card repayment	R 2 500.00
Debts repayments	R 500.00
Cell phones	R 1 500.00
Education	R 2 200.00
Rates and taxes	R 700.00
Water	R 500.00
Electricity	R 800.00
Clothes and shoes	R 1 500.00
Groceries	R 5 000.00
Entertainment	R 1 000.00
Stokvels	R 1 200.00
Transport	R 4 000.00
Insurance	R 1 200.00
Donations paid	R 5 000.00
Television subscription	R 800.00
Security	R 500.00
Employees' salaries	R 3 000.00
Savings and investments	R 1 000.00

Horizontal format of a family budget
Budget of Motloung family for June 2020

Income			Expenditure		
Salaries	35 000	00	Car repayment	6 500	00
Rent income	7 500	00	Groceries	5 000	00
Profit	4 500	00	Donations paid	5 000	00
Interest income	2 000	00	Transport	4 000	00
			Furniture repayment	4 000	00
			Employees' salaries	3 000	00
			Credit card repayment	2 500	00
			Education	2 200	00
			Long-term loans repayment	1 800	00
			Cellphones	1 500	00
			Clothes and shoes	1 500	00
			Short-term loans repayment	1 200	00
			Insurance	1 200	00
			Stokvels	1 200	00
			Savings and investment	1 000	00
			Entertainment	1 000	00
			Television subscription	800	00
			Electricity	800	00
			Rates and taxes	700	00
			Water	500	00
			Debts repayment	500	00
			Security	500	00
Total income	**49 000**	**00**	**Total expenditure**	**46 400**	**00**
Net surplus				**2 600**	**00**

Vertical format of a family budget
Budget of Motloung family for June 2020

Income			49 000	00
Salaries	35 000	00		
Rent income	7 500	00		
Profit	4 500	00		
Interest income	2 000	00		
Expenditure			**46 400**	**00**
Car repayment	6 500	00		
Groceries	5 000	00		
Donations paid	5 000	00		
Transport	4 000	00		
Furniture repayment	4 000	00		
Employees' salaries	3 000	00		
Credit card repayment	2 500	00		
Education	2 200	00		
Long-term loans repayment	1 800	00		
Cellphones	1 500	00		
Clothes and shoes	1 500	00		
Short-term loans repayment	1 200	00		
Insurance	1 200	00		
Stokvels	1 200	00		
Savings and investment	1 000	00		
Entertainment	1 000	00		
Television subscription	800	00		
Electricity	800	00		
Rates and taxes	700	00		
Water	500	00		
Debts repayment	500	00		
Security	500	00		
Net surplus			**2 600**	**00**

Vertical format of a family budget using a single column

Budget of Motloung family for June 2020

Income	49 000	00
Salaries	35 000	00
Rent income	7 500	00
Profit	4 500	00
Interest income	2 000	00
Expenditure	**46 400**	**00**
Car repayment	6 500	00
Groceries	5 000	00
Donations paid	5 000	00
Transport	4 000	00
Furniture repayment	4 000	00
Employees' salaries	3 000	00
Credit card repayment	2 500	00
Education	2 200	00
Long-term loans repayment	1 800	00
Cell phones	1 500	00
Clothes and shoes	1 500	00
Short-term loans repayment	1 200	00
Insurance	1 200	00
Stokvels	1 200	00
Savings and investment	1 000	00
Entertainment	1 000	00
Television subscription	800	00
Electricity	800	00
Rates and taxes	700	00
Water	500	00
Debts repayment	500	00
Security	500	00
Net surplus	**2 600**	**00**

(Formats adapted from Msimanga, 2016)

As you can see, the budget of the Motloung family shows a surplus of R 2 600.00. The family can decide to keep the amount for emergencies or use some of the money to pay off some of its debts. There are many lessons which can be learnt from the family budget presented above such as, which expenditure can be targeted for reduction to achieve financial sustainability. In the above formats, a budget is presented by starting with the highest source of income to the lowest source of income and the highest expenditure to the lowest expenditure. This helps a family to identify its main sources of income and to identify which expenditure takes more from the family budget. This can be used for better planning income and expenditure. Another approach of presenting a family budget can be done by presenting regular income and fixed expenditure first. The format used will depend on families' preferences because the formats are not ultimately that important; rather, the income and expenditure is important.

4.5   Conclusion

This chapter focused on preparation of a family budgeting as a financial planning strategy of a family. In order to prepare a family budget, family income (net) and family expenditure (excluding stop order payments) were discussed as main components of a family budget. Steps in preparing a family budget were discussed and finally, a family budget was presented. It was highlighted that a family budget is prepared on a monthly basis, but it will be helpful if the family monthly budgets are prepared in advance for the whole year. It was also highlighted that a family budget can clearly indicate the expenditure that must be targeted to achieve financial sustainability. The next chapter will look at family financial plans organisation, implementation and control.

CHAPTER
5

5.1 Introduction

The previous chapter dealt with family budgeting as part of the financial plan of a family. In this chapter, financial process which different families can put in place to organise family finances are discussed as well as implementation of family financial processes. Lastly, family financial processes control is discussed. The context of 'family members' in this chapter is mainly parents. The next section discusses family financial processes organisation.

5.2 Family financial processes organisation

Different families have different approaches towards organising their finances. The approach adopted by the family will determine how the financial processes of a family are organised. Families can adopt either separate funds utilisation of joint funds utilisation. Both approaches have implications on how a family will approach its finances.

5.2.1 Separate funds utilisation approach

Separate funds utilisation approach is a family funds management approach in which different members of a family are responsible for their own funds but are allocated family financial responsibilities. Members of the family are free to spend their money on anything they want as long as they play their part in their assigned family financial responsibilities. A family member can decide to buy a car, and no one will question him/her as long as he/she do not default on agreed family financial responsibilities. This approach is not suitable for families who are married in civil marriage better known as community of property because those people are jointly liable for each other's debts and jointly own each other's property. The actions of one partner can negatively affect the finances of another partner.

One member of the family can spend his/her money on things that do not accumulate wealth but benefit from the wealth accumulated by other members of the family. An example of this is someone who will spend money on entertainment and parties without considering buying a bed. Other members of the family will buy a bed for a family house which will be used by the person who spend his/her money on other things. This hinders family progress and other members of the family suffer because of the actions of that one family member.

In some instances, one family member will have the responsibility of paying for things which do not accumulate value such as clothes, groceries and pocket monies, while the other family member will have the responsibility of buying a car, household equipment and furniture. When there are conflicts in the family (as families are prone to conflicts), the latter family member will boast that all the assets of the family belong to him/her. It will be truth in the eyes of everyone because the things that the first family member spent money on cannot be seen at a later stage. This deepens the conflict because one person proudly shows what he/she did in the past years while the other person cannot show anything, but the person was loyal in meeting his/her family financial responsibilities. You will find a situation whereby even young children in the family will tell you, 'This is my father's/mother's lounge suite'. Relatives and family friends will know who owns what in the family and the other family member who does not own anything feel robbed and that can also cause family problems. The alternative to this approach is joint funds utilisation.

5.2.2 Joint funds utilisation approach

Joint funds utilisation approach is a family funds management approach in which family members' income belongs to the family and family members are only given pocket money for their own use. A joint family budget is drawn based on family members' income. One family member is given the responsibility of managing the family finances. This family member should be able to communicate, show responsibility and be accountable, as discussed in Chapter One. In this approach family, members (including children) are given their pocket money to cater for their personal needs such as entertainment. This teaches family members (including children) to spend wisely.

In this approach, all the expenditures of a family are included in the family budget. No member of a family can use family income to buy anything that was not budgeted for in the family budget, but a family member can use his/her pocket money to do so. The amount allocated as pocket money should include money for buying clothes and shoes. Families should decide on how to handle the needs of extended family members. The needs of extended family members can be catered for by either allocating a certain amount of money from a family budget to cater for such needs or each person will use his/her pocket money to cater for such needs. The problem of using a persons' pocket money is that one family member might not meet the needs of his/her extended family members while the other one is able to meet them. If this happens, it will appear as if the needs of one extended family member/s are catered for, while the needs of another extended family member/s are neglected. This might cause conflicts with and among extended families.

Purchases of cars, equipment, furniture and other assets cannot be made by individuals but should be based on the family financial plans. In this approach there is no family member who can claim ownership of particular assets of the family because all the assets are purchased from the family income and not from an individual's income. Family members cannot raise loans or create debts without the approval of the family because that will have an impact on family financial plans and family credit scores for joint credit application. This approach will be more applicable where people are married in community of property because they jointly own the assets and are jointly liable for debts. The next sections are based on this approach.

5.3 Family financial processes implementation

Family financial processes implementation is the process of putting into action or practice all the decisions of the family related to the finances. It would be a waste of time for families to have financial structures, prepare a statement of net worth, have good long-term, medium-term and short-term family financial plans and a good family budget if they are not put anything into action or practise it. The qualities of the person who manages the finances of the family are very important in this process. It is the responsibility of that person to communicate all the financial decisions of the family to other family members. The person is responsible for ensuring that family finances are used as per family financial plans and family budget. Necessary payments should be made on time and all budget items should be purchased on time. The person responsible for managing family finances should account to the family members about the usage of the finances.

5.4 Family financial processes control

Family financial processes control involves ensuring that all financial processes of the family are in line with family decisions. Control process checks compliance to financial plans. This process takes place when the person who manages the finances of the family accounts to the family members. Deviations from the financial plans are identified and revised for approval. Lastly, this process identifies whether there is a need to review the financial plans and make recommendations on reviews.

5.5 Conclusion

This chapter dealt with family finances organisation. Two approaches which families can adopt to organise their finances are discussed as, separate funds utilisation approach and joint funds utilisation approach. Different scenarios are discussed on applicability of both approaches. It is highlighted that joint funds utilisation approach is more relevant for people married in community of property. The section discussed the importance of implementation of financial plans by the person who manages the finances of the family. Lastly, control of family finances is discussed. The importance of communication, responsibility and accountability is emphasised. The next chapter looks into causes of financial problems in families.

CHAPTER

6

THE CAUSES OF FINANCIAL PROBLEMS IN FAMILIES AND DEALING WITH IDENTIFIED PROBLEMS

6.1 Introduction

The previous chapter focused on family financial processes of organisation, implementation, and control. In this chapter, the causes of financial problems in families are identified and discussed. This chapter tries to address how to deal with identified causes of financial problems in the family. Suggestions on how to deal with identified financial problems are discussed.

6.2 Premarital debts

Premarital debts are debts that married people had accumulated before entering into a marriage contract. Some people have already accumulated large premarital debts and a lot of family money is spent on these debts. This causes family financial problems because family money is spent on financing these debts instead of focusing on building family's financial stability.

It would be wise for people to repay their debts before entering a marriage contract. Families should discuss how to address premarital debts if they were not settled prior to the marriage. A debt management plan to pay off these debts must be prepared.

6.3 Financing the needs of extended families

Financing the needs of extended families refers to the situation whereby a family is supporting their extended families financially. It is common practice in some communities for a family to finance the needs of their extended family. This causes family financial problems when it doesn't happen because a family should share its income with extended families.

Families should have a plan on how to finance the needs of extended families as discussed in Chapter Five. If families know how to finance the needs of extended family members, they will be able to budget for those needs. Extended family members should know how far financial support will go, so that they know that they cannot get all the money they want but they will get a certain amount of money to finance certain needs. This makes it easier for the family to avoid financial problems.

6.4   Unequal income

Unequal income is when the income family members is not the same, which is normally the case. This causes financial problems when a family member who earns a higher income wants to contribute the same amount contributed by other members of the family who earn less income. In some cases, a family member who earns a lower income is not prepared to contribute because he/she feels that his/her income is less and should be used for other things.

Family members should put the collective needs (needs of a family) ahead of their personal needs and stick to family financial plans. Family members should contribute progressively to the financial wellbeing of the family. This means family members who earn a higher income should contribute more and those earning a lower income should contribute lesser. Family members should contribute in proportion to their income.

6.5   No one taking the lead on finances

Family members might want to work together on family finances but are unable to do so because there is no one from the family who raises this issue. In other cases, when this matter has been raised, no one is prepared to take the lead because people do not want to take responsibility and do not want to account. If there is no one taking a leadership role with regard to family finances, there will be problems with the family finances.

One person from the family should raise the issue of working together as family members on family finances. The person might be surprised by the way other family members will positively respond to the proposal of working together on family finances. Some family members might indicate that they had the same idea but did not know how to propose it. When family members have agreed to start working together, they should choose one member of the family who will lead the process. The person to be chosen is not necessarily the one who suggested the idea, but it should be someone who meets leadership qualities as discussed in Chapter One.

6.6   Non-contribution by some members of the family

In some families there is the challenge of family members who do not comply with the family arrangements, by not contributing as expected. Some family members will contribute only a part of the expected contribution. Non-contribution by some family members might be due to family members prioritising their personal commitments over family commitments. Non-contribution or partial contribution by family means that the family will be unable to meet its expenditure. All these forms of non-contribution by family members cause family financial problems.

All members of the family should contribute as the family agreed. The person who manages the finances of the family should talk to the person who default on contribution. If that fails other family members should be informed about the problem. There should be family rules on how to deal with people who default on contributions as discussed in Chapter One.

6.7 Lack of transparency about the finances

Lack of transparency about the finances is a situation whereby family members are not given information about the status of family finances. This is caused by lack of communication about family finances. People who contribute to family income do not know how their money is used or whether it is used to pay for budget items. When there is no transparency about how family money is used, family members think that the family has a lot of money and at times become reluctant to contribute. Some family members are not sure whether the person who manages family funds also contributes as expected and suspect that this person might be using family money for his or her personal benefit.

It is important that the person who deals with family finances should account on family income received and family expenditure. This will put other family members on board with the finances of a family. Family members will know when there is a need for additional contributions.

6.8 Lack of savings and investments

Families do not save and invest money when their income is less than their expenditure. This creates financial problems because in cases of emergency, there is no money available to finance the emergency. Therefore, families take out loans to finance their emergencies. Other families take out loans to pay for luxuries.

Savings and investments can help families to access funds when they need them for various reasons. In times of emergencies, the family can use their savings. It is important for families to save and invest money to buy luxury goods. Patience should be practised with regard to buying luxury goods. Families should save and invest money for parties, weddings, and holidays. They should not organise such functions and activities if they have not saved money to fund them.

6.9 Impulsive spending and spontaneous competition

Impulsive spending it is when family members spend money without giving a thought about the expenditure. This happens when family members buy things because they see them and want them, even if they do not need them. Spontaneous competition takes place when family members compete with other people or other family in an unplanned manner. A family member will notice that someone bought something, and the family member then wants to own the same item. This leads to family members owning a number of things that they do not use because these things were bought for no reason. In many instances' family members will not have money and they will buy on credit using store credit cards and credit cards and that is when their financial problems start.

This can be managed if family members have financial plans and stick to them. Family members should buy things that they need and should plan before buying such items. Members can save a lot of money if they avoid impulsive spending and spontaneous competition. They can avoid debts because they will only buy the things they planned to buy. People should avoid buying things due to the influence of marketing.

6.10 Overspending

Overspending occurs when family members spend more money than they have. Buying on credit, for example, is spending money that a person does not have and that is overspending. Availability of credit makes other family members overspend and buy because they are given credit. The use of credit has contributed a great deal to people overspending. You will hear people boasting that their credit limit (which they normally refer to as buying slip) has been increased or is high; the next things is that they spend money that they do not have.

Family members should not spend money they do not have. People should avoid stores credit cards and credit cards. People should understand that credit is not money they have but it is a strategy of credit granters to allow people to overspend. People should save for the things they want to buy.

6.11   Over-indebtedness

Over-indebtedness is a situation that prevails when family members have more debts and cannot afford to repay them. Over-indebtedness makes family members struggle financially and be unable to contribute to family finances. Other family members will not feel happy about the situation because they would have sacrificed some of the things to be able to meet family financial expectations.

This problem should not be ignored as if it will just disappear because it would persist if it not dealt with. Therefore, a debt management plan should be developed as discussed in Chapter Three to help a family member to become debt free. Family members should sacrifice certain things or postpone purchases of other things to help the family member become debt free. Family members should also use their personal skills to generate income which can be used to finance the debts of a family.

6.12   Natural disasters and pandemics

Natural disasters are catastrophes which are brought by nature such as tornados, tsunamis, and floods. Pandemics are diseases that affect the whole world and the most recent pandemic is COVID-19. Natural disasters and pandemics cause financial problems for families because families change their lifestyles during these times. Families change how they live daily to avoid being affected. During the time of COVID-19 families incurred unplanned expenditure such as buying face masks and sanitizers while the prices of other goods and services were increasing. Some families could not afford to provide for their needs and wants because some of them did not earn an income during this period.

Families should save and invest money that they can use when there are natural disasters and pandemics. Instead of raising loans, families should plan how they can use money saved from other expenditure to finance new expenditure. The money that was used for transport can be used to buy more groceries, for example.

6.13 Economic conditions

'Economic conditions' refers to whether the economy is in the upswing or downswing. During an economic upswing, technically people will have money while during an economic downswing, technically people will not have sufficient money and will therefore normally struggle financially. Some of the economic indicators used to determine the economic conditions are interest rates, exchange rates and inflation rates. If the interest rates are high families that have more debts will encounter financial problems. If the rate of exchange of a country's currency is lower than that of other countries families will encounter financial problems because the imports will be expensive. If the inflation rate is high, families will encounter financial problems because the prices of goods and services will be high. During the times of COVID-19 the economy was not performing well and the rate of exchange of South Africa reached its lowest; interest rates were reduced but were still high and the inflation rate increased. All this caused family financial problems for families; therefore, families should save and invest money to cater for unfavourable economic conditions.

6.14 Conclusion

This chapter dealt with some of the issues which causes financial problems for families. It also suggested ways of overcoming these financial problems. The chapter highlighted that financial problems of a family can be overcome by preparing financial plans, savings, and investments. The importance of sticking to financial plans is emphasised. The next chapter discusses practical tips that families can use to save some money.

CHAPTER
7

PRACTICAL WAYS OF SAVING SOME MONEY

7.1   Introduction

The previous chapter identified some of causes of financial problems for families. The chapter suggested some of the ways of overcoming the identified causes. This final chapter of the book focuses on practical ways in which families can save some money. The next section deals with how money can be saved by buying property instead of renting property.

7.2   Buy a property instead of renting property

Families should try to buy a property instead of renting it. When the property is rented, the money paid is an expense and does not add any value towards the investment portfolio of a family nor accumulate value. Simply put, it is money gone. When a property is purchased, the property belongs to the family and its value might appreciate over time to the benefit of the family. A property purchased by a family is an asset and can be sold at a later stage. It is better to buy a property than to rent it because the rental amount paid for apartments is nearly the same as the bond instalment amount.

7.3   Insure property and assets

Insuring property and assets are done by paying monthly premiums for protection against future loses. It is important for families to insure their property and assets against future loses. Insurance cover saves families a great deal of money in the event of insured loses. It is important for families to review insurance covers regularly to ensure that the cover is sufficient, to avoid underinsurance. Also, families should also not over-insure their property because they will only be reimbursed to the maximum value of the insured risk. Insurance covers for items that can be easily replaced, or that are cheaper to replace should be avoided. Instead families should create a savings account for such replacements.

7.4 Save on electricity

Electricity is one of the recurring monthly expenditures and the way electricity is used affects the finances of a family. Experts usually warn that a geyser is one of the home appliances with high electricity consumption. Reducing electricity consumption from a geyser can save a family money. The lessons I have learnt during load-shedding periods was that I have wasted a lot of money over years by switching on the geyser for twenty-four hours every day instead of switching it on for not more than three hours per day. Switching the geyser on for about three hour per day saved my family about 30% of electricity expenditure in summer and 33.3% in winter. Checking the geyser temperature settings saved my family an additional 15% on electricity expenditure. The amount saved from electricity expenditure after applying geyser controls could have been a good investment if geyser controls were applied many years ago. It is important for families to check geyser temperature settings and switch the geyser on and off when necessary.

7.5 Compare prices of different stores

The prices of products are not the same at competing stores and families can save a lot of money if they can compare the prices before they buy; this fact is supported by Surveys done on prices charged by different stores. In the long run the amounts saved per item can save families a great deal of money. The difference in prices of different items might be low but when those amounts are added together over a year, it can save families a lot of money.

7.6 Take advantage of discounts and sales promotions

A discount is a reduction on a selling price when goods are purchased or when stores sell goods at a lower price than the normal price. There are times when stores offer a certain percentage of discount on purchases. These discount ranges from around 20% up to 75%. If a person pays only 25% of the original price of goods that is a great saving. These discounts should not be ignored because a lot of money can be saved if the discounts are offered on goods worth hundreds and thousands of Rands. Many grocery stores issue their discount catalogues and pamphlets on a regular basis. Families should check these discounts and plan where to buy; if these discounts are added together a family can save a lot of money which can be used to buy other things.

Sales promotion takes place when the business wants to increase sales of a particular product by giving special offers. Different stores offer discounts to customers when they spend in a particular manner. Sales promotion can take place when the stores offer the third item for free if three products are purchased or when the stores offers the second item at a discounted rate when two of the same items or brands are purchased. Families can save money by paying for two products instead of three products or paying less for the second product. Thousands of Rands can be saved in a year if all the amounts saved are added together.

7.7   Buy in bulk

Buying in bulk means that goods are bought in large quantities as a package. It is cheaper to buy in bulk because the stores normally charge a lower price per item for goods bought in bulk compared to items purchased in small quantities. Non-perishable items can be bought in bulk to be used over a longer period. Goods that can be easily kept for future use can be purchased in bulk to get the benefits of buying in bulk and to avoid the price increase. Families can save money over a period of time by buying in bulk instead of buying in small quantities.

7.8   Practise speculative buying

Speculative buying is when a person waits for prices of products to drop before buying the products. Speculative buying can save a family money when it buys the product after there has been a price drop. Families should understand different price trends in the market to understand when to buy from a particular store. A popular way of speculative buying is when families buy winter clothes at the end of winter because the prices drop. Stores are not prepared to keep the winter stock for the next winter season. It will be cheaper to buy certain goods (except school uniform and school stationery) in January than to buy them in December. In December, stores want to maximise their profits when people have extra money from bonuses and savings. In January, the purchasing power of the people is low; businesses use promotions to get a share of sales. Families can save money by delaying their purchases on the days between December and January.

7.9   Use of reward cards and membership rewards

Reward cards are store cards given to customers to earn points on purchases or when they use the card at business partners a store. Most reward cards are freely offered, and some are offered for a nominal fee. Some businesses offer special discounts to reward only the cardholders, thus it is important for family members to get rewards cards especially if they are available for free. Some reward cards give cardholders cashback to spend. When discount amounts and cashback amounts are added together, a family can save more money in a year. These savings can be used for other purposes.

Membership rewards are rewards that are enjoyed by people who belong to a reward programme which is mainly paid for by the store issuing the reward cards. Families can take memberships offered by different organisations but should ensure that the benefits supersede the costs. In most cases the benefits are attractive and can save families money.

7.10   Book for holidays in advance

Families who plan to go on a holiday should plan. Booking holiday accommodation and flights some months in advance can save a family more money. Holiday accommodation and flights are cheaper when the demand is not yet determined and when demand increases, accommodation and flights become expensive. A family can spend half the amount they would have spent on holidays by booking in advance. Booking accommodation and flights around March for December and early January holidays can save families thousands of Rands. Money saved from accommodation and flights can be used to cover other expenses during the holidays. This is normally applicable when direct bookings are done.

7.11   Avoid the influence of marketing

Marketing refers to the strategies used by businesses to encourage people to by their products or use the services they offer. One of the marketing strategies that businesses use is telemarketing. Telemarketing takes place when people receive unsolicited calls from businesses inviting them to buy their products or use their services. Normally telemarketers are persuasive and strategic in their approach which makes many people to end up buying the products and services they do not need. A good example is a number of people who own many cell phones which some people are still paying for and which are not necessary. Another example is that of family members investing money in schemes that are not known simply because they were invited to invest. The two scenarios emanate from telemarketing and family members can save money if they can avoid unplanned expenditure created by telemarketing.

7.12   Check till slips and card payment slips

It is important that till slips and card payment slips are checked after making a payment. There are stores which put certain prices on the shelves for products but when a payment is made at the till point, the amount is higher. Normally businesses will charge the price that the customer has seen and that can save money. Checking card payment slips is important because I have had the experience at two well-known restaurants where I was charged more money to increase the tip of the waitresses (done by two ladies at different restaurants). I only checked the card payment slips when I was at home and that was a loss; fortunately, it was not thousands of Rands. If all small amounts of money lost are be added together over a period of time it can be a great loss.

7.13 Compare bank charges from different banks

Bank charges are amounts charged by banks for the use of their services such as deposits and withdrawals. Different banks have different charges for their services. Comparison of amounts charged by different banks will help family members to get better offers. Lower bank charges will amount to greater savings in the long run.

7.14 Check bank statements

Bank statements should be regularly checked for transactions that are foreign or not recognised. There are companies which deduct small amounts of money from the bank accounts of family members and at times cell phone notifications are not received and people lose money. When these small amounts are added together, they can make a great loss. I have seen a bank statements of someone who lost little amounts of money over two and a half years because the bank statement was not checked. If the money lost was invested, it could have saved a family money, or a family could have used that money to finance its needs.

7.15 Compare interest rates

Interest rate it is the rate charged on borrowed money or the rate of return on investment. Comparison of interest rates charged, and interest rates offered can make great savings or good returns. When borrowing money, it is important to be borrow from a place with lower interest rate charges because the cost of the debt will therefore be lower. When investing money, it is important to get the highest interest rate possible in order to get higher returns on that investment. A difference of one percent over a long period of time is a lot of money, therefore it is important to compare the rates of interest charged and offered.

7.16 Avoid quick cash investments and pyramid schemes

Quick cash investments are investments which promise people high returns on investment within a short period of time. Families should avoid quick cash investment because it is not possible for return on investment to be high in the short run because financial institutions use invested funds to lend them to debtors who will pay a higher interest rate. This makes it impossible to receive quick high returns; thus, a number of people have lost their money in such schemes.

Pyramid schemes are investment schemes where people who invest money earn returns on their investment when they have recruited a certain number of investors who will push them up in the pyramid. Families should avoid investing in pyramid schemes because the first people who invest are the ones who benefit, and the last ones suffer a loss. Families should invest their money with registered investment houses and practise patience to get the returns.

7.17 Start saving small amounts of money

Saving money takes a lot of sacrifice, therefore, it must not be seen as a burden. If saving money becomes a burden people dumps the plan quickly. Saving money should start with saving small amounts on regular basis up until saving money is a norm. The amount saved should be increased over a period as more cash becomes available. The amount invested can become handy in the long run, but the skill of saving will help families to be able to save for the things they need. Saving money is one of the best strategies that family members can use to achieve financial sustainability.

7.18   Conclusion

This chapter discussed some of the ideas that families and family members can use to save some money. The practical ways discussed have been tested and proven. The ways of saving money discussed in this chapter are: buying a property instead of renting it; insuring property and assets; saving on electricity; comparing the prices of different stores, taking advantage of discounts and sales promotions, buying in bulks and using speculative buying; belonging to rewards programmes; booking holidays in advance; guarding against the influence of marketing; checking till slips, card payment slips and bank statements; comparing bank charges and interest rates; avoiding quick cash investments and pyramid schemes; and start to save by saving small amounts of money on regular basis. These suggested ways of saving money can be used strategically by families to help them gain financial sustainability.

CHAPTER

8

UNDERSTANDING ISSUES WHICH HAVE FINANCIAL
IMPACT ON MIDDLE CLASS, LOW CLASS AND THE
UNEMPLOYED

8.1   Introduction

The previous chapter focused on practical ways of saving money. This
final chapter of the book focuses on issues that have a financial impact
on families. The identified issues are discussed because they affect
families in different classes differently. These issues affect the middle
classes, lower classes and the unemployed more than people in higher
classes. It is important for people who are mostly affected by these issues
to understand them, in order to be able to respond appropriately. Most
of these issues are known by family members but they do not know how
the issues impact their finances. The next sections discuss how the
identified issues impact middle class, low class and the unemployed
financially.

8.2   Demand and supply

Demand refers to the quantities of goods which are needed to be
purchased at a given price and given time. When the demand for a
particular product is high, the price of a product increases and when the
demand for a particular product is low, the price of a product decreases.
A good example that can be used is that of a fuel price. During the
lockdown which was enforced in South Africa during the time of
COVID-19, the movement of South Africans was restricted and that
reduced their demand for fuel. Due to a decrease in demand for fuel the
price of fuel was low; in fact, it was the lowest price we had paid for fuel
in a long time. When the lockdown was eased the price of fuel slightly
increased because people started to travel and the demand for fuel

slightly increased. When the lockdown reached level three and the economy started opening there was a high increase in the price of fuel because the demand for fuel was that much higher. Another example is that hotel room prices: the prices of hotel rooms are high during peak season because of high demand and the prices are low during off-peak season because of low demand. Families should understand the influence of demand on the price in order for them to know when they should spend to take advantage of the low prices.

Supply refers to the quantities of products offered for sale at a given price and given time. When the supply of a particular product is high, the price of that product decreases and when the supply of a product is low, the price of that product increases. Normally, there is an inverse relationship between supply and price. When suppliers have more stock at their disposal to sell, they reduce the price of the products in stock. This leads to businesses selling their products at a lower price which is normally known as "sale" – discussed previously. When the suppliers are only able to supply a few products, they increase their prices because more people compete for fewer products. A good example is when the business sells exclusive goods: they supply few goods and charge high prices. Families should understand the influence of supply on the price in order to make sure they buy when the price is low.

8.3   Imports and exports

Imports are the goods and services that are bought from other countries. When people buy the imported goods, the demand for similar locally produced goods will decrease and that will lead to reduced production. When production is reduced, people who work in such industries might lose their jobs and that will increase unemployment. It is important for local people to support campaigns such as the "Proudly South Africa" campaign. When families buy South African products, they increase the demand for locally produced goods and the increase in demand will lead to increase in production of such goods. Increase in production can create more employment opportunities. When more employment opportunities are created a demand for more goods is created which leads to a multiplier effect (proportion of increase in income as a result of injection or a small change in input that leads to a larger change in output). Multiplier effect can change the economy altogether and economic growth will be achieved with all its benefits. This cycle can help families benefit more if it continues, therefore, when family members decide to buy, they should prioritise locally produced products to bring a change in the local economy.

Exports are goods and services that are produced in a country but are sold to other countries. When a country sells its products to other countries it will have a wider market for the products and the demand for its products will be high. When the demand for locally produced products is high, production will be increased and an increase in production will create employment opportunities. When employment opportunities are created families can benefit and that can also lead to a multiplier effect. The economy will benefit as earlier discussed.

8.4   Rate of exchange

This is the rate at which the currency of one country is exchanged for the currency of another country. This is normally presented at the end of news bulletins and on economic news, where they will show $1 = R 17. 07. It means if a South African has R 1 707.00 and visits United States, the person will only get $ 100. If South Africans buy goods from United States, the goods will be expensive but when Americans buy goods from South Africa the goods will be cheaper. Foreign tourists visit South Africa because they spend less during their holidays in South Africa. It will be very expensive for South African to visit America and this might be one of the reasons that few South Africans (middle class, low class and unemployed) have ever visited such countries. When I visited Botswana five years ago, I saw how the rate of Pula 1 to R 1.24 a negative impact on my budget had because for every Pula 1 000.00 I spent I had to add R 240.00. The situation is getting worse as Pula 1 is around R 1.46 in July 2020, therefore, for every Pula 1 000.00 spent, an additional R 460.00 is needed. Understanding how the rates of exchange work can help family members to make sound financial decisions with regard to international transactions.

8.5   Fuel price

In South Africa, the fuel price is controlled by government and is determined monthly. Fuel prices affect families negatively if the fuel price is high and South Africa's fuel prices are high because they include several taxes. The fuel prices in Lesotho are very low compared to the prices charged in South Africa. When the price of fuel increases, it affects the cost of other services such as transport and the price of goods. Transport fares increase to ensure that service providers do not run at a loss. Transport is also used to move goods to different places and some manufacturing equipment needs fuel, therefore, an increase in fuel price increases the price of the products. Families should know the effect of the monthly fuel announcement on their budget because it affects them in various ways.

8.6   Interest rate

Interest rate is the amount of money charged by creditors on credit granted. Interest rate is dependent on a repo rate (a rate the reserve bank charges to the banks for credit granted). If the repo rate is decreased, the interest rate will also decrease. If the interest rate is reduced, the cost of credit becomes cheaper. Families that owe money will save when the interest rate is reduced. In the year 2020, the interest rate reached the lowest it has been in a very long time. This was due to several reductions which were announced as a way of bringing some relief to people who had debts. People who had debts saved more money on interest and that means they had more money available. People with fixed interest rates did not benefit from these reductions. The money that family members save from reduced interest rates can be used for other purposes and help towards settling debts earlier.

8.7   Inflation

Inflation is a general increase in the prices of goods and services over a period of time. The results of inflation are the loss of purchasing power of money which means the money that people have can only buy less of what was previously purchased. For example, an amount of R 100.00 cannot buy even half of things that it could purchase ten years ago, due to inflation. Families should know that inflation shrinks the purchasing power of their income; thus, the fact that when salary increases are negotiated, inflation rate is a key factor. If the inflation rate is at 5% and the employees get a 5% salary increase, there is no real increase because the increase will be used to cover the inflation. When family members take investments, they are normally advised to take an annual policy increase to cover inflation because the value of the investment which does not cover inflation will be reduced in years to come.

8.8   Taxes

Taxes are compulsory monies paid to the government by individuals and legal entities as imposed on income or on spending. Taxes are categorised into direct tax (tax charged on income) and indirect tax (tax charged when spending). When income tax, which is tax charged on income increases, families' disposable income decreases and that will affect their budget. When Value Added Tax (VAT) was increased from 14% to 15%, families paid more for taxable goods and services and their buying power was reduced. Paying for toll roads including introduction of e-tolls increases people's tax burden and that affects their spending power because they will have to spend more on transport costs. Family members should understand that when income tax is reduced, they will get additional income but if it is increased, their income is reduced. Increase in VAT has more impact on the middle class, low class and the unemployed than it does on the richer classes. The same applies to paying toll-fees and e-tolls, the amount paid does not have any significant impact on the high class compared to other classes and the unemployed.

8.9   No-fee schools and free higher education

No-fee schools are schools which, according to the South African Schools Act, are not supposed to charge school fees. Learners in such schools are provided with all learning support materials. Parents are not expected to pay for learners to access education. No-fee schools affect parents negatively when schools introduce several strategies which will require parents to pay on regular basis and which, in real terms, is tantamount to a fee paying at a no-fee school. Parents should not agree to pay for learning support materials and weekly fees needed by such schools because the practice affects poor families negatively. During parents' meetings at these schools, such issues should be voted against.

Free higher education is when the students whose parents or guardians fall within a certain threshold can access higher education without paying any fees. Students' fees are paid for by National Student Financial Aid Scheme (NSFAS). This affects families positively because they can use the money that would have been used for higher education to finance other needs of the family. Families should encourage children who are about to enter higher education to apply for this financial aid scheme.

8.10   Infrastructure development and hosting of events

Infrastructure development refers to projects undertaken to improve infrastructure in a country. Infrastructure development can include, amongst others, building of public goods, and repairs of public goods. Infrastructure development can stimulate the economy in the short and the long run. Family members are positively affected during the implementation of projects because they can get employment opportunities and those who sell goods can increase their income as more money will be available. Income accumulated during project implementation can be used to finance the family needs and some families benefit after project completion when the infrastructure is open to the public.

Hosting of events need infrastructure development and families can enjoy the benefits of infrastructure development in preparation for hosting an event. One of the well-known events hosted in South Africa was the soccer World Cup, hosted in the year 2010 and the infrastructure developed during that time is still beneficial to South African citizens. When the sporting events, concerts, conferences, and other events are hosted, people in that area benefit from the influx of non-residents in their area. The influx of non-residents in a particular area is an economic booster for the local economy. Countries spend money to bid for hosting international events because they know that hosting of such events will boost the economy. South African cities have started to make proposals to host sports events like soccer cup finals. Sometimes, the supporters do not understand why many such events are taken to certain areas but one of the reasons is that municipalities in those areas spend money to bring the events to that area, knowing that the event will be an economic stimulator. Families should take advantage of generating income from events hosted in their area. This can be in a form of temporary employment or providing a service or selling products.

8.11 Corruption

Corruption refers to different forms of dishonesty by people who are in different positions of power of authority. The focus of this section will be on fraud, bribes, money laundering and fronting. Fraud is a form of corruption which involves deceiving people aiming at personal gain and it normally happens in the form of misrepresentation. One form of fraud is when people are asked to invest a certain amount of money, promised high returns and at the end, they lose everything. A bribe is payment in cash or in kind to a person who has an influence on something that can give you a personal benefit. One form of bribery is when people are promised jobs and pay in any form to be employed. Some people end up not being employed and their money is not returned, or the favour is not returned. Another form of bribery is when people are awarded contracts that they do not deserve and in return they make a payment. The payment is referred to as "kick-backs" and that leads to money laundering. Money laundering is when the origin of money which is illegally acquired is covered. One of the popular forms of money laundering is known as a "brown envelope" because it is alleged that in South Africa, money generated through corruption changes hands through a brown envelope because it cannot be deposited at the bank for obvious reasons. Another form of corruption is fronting, which takes place when employees or people without power are registered as owners of businesses by the rightful owners to get contracts which are specified for certain designated groups. Most of the times people who are used as "fronts" do not know that they do not benefit from their ownership of the business.

Fraudsters normally take the money of people who need it and that affect their finances negatively as some people raise loans to invest in fraudulent schemes. Some people raise loans to pay bribes and end up not getting anything in return. People who obtain contracts fraudulently pay kickbacks and at times that makes them run at a loss. Money laundering affects the finances of families because it leads to inflated prices which are borne by other people. When people are fronting, they lose in their promised share of the profits and that affect their finances because they could be making more money.

People should not engage in corruption because it has a negative impact on the finances of the families. People should not invest money in unknown schemes, and they should avoid paying bribes. It is important for corrupt activities to be reported to police as it is crime and is against humanity. People might think that corruption does not affect them, but it affects some people directly and some people indirectly, as discussed above.

8.12 Price fixing (collusion)

Price fixing or collusion occurs when suppliers of a particular product or service agree to increase the price that they charge. Price fixing or collusion become effective when all role players in the supply of a product or service participate because if others do not participate, consumers will buy from non-participating suppliers as their prices will be low. Price fixing or collusion happened during the period leading up to the 2010 Soccer World Cup which was hosted in South Africa because suppliers saw the event to maximise their profits. A good example that affected me was the price of cement because I was involved in a building project. When I started the project in 2006 the price of cement was around R 48.00 and when I completed the project in 2007 the price of cement was around R 72.00 which was an unbelievable price increase of R 24.00. In 2017, the price of cement was still around R 72.00 which was ten years later. The competition tribunal found out that there was a price fixing or collusion by cement suppliers, and they were fined. This is just one example of such activities and they take place in different sectors.

Price fixing or collusion affect families negatively because they pay higher prices and lose a lot of money in the process. Based on the example given above, 1 000 bags of cement at R 48.00 each will have a total cost of R 48 000.00, whereas, at R 72.00 each the total cost will be R 72 000.00 which is a loss of R 24 000.00. Consumers are not reimbursed when the price fixers or colluders pay a fine. Family members should be careful of abnormal price increases and report suspected cases to the competition tribunal for investigation. This can save families a lot of money. Such tendencies emerged when COVID-19 was encountered in South Africa: the prices of sanitisers and face masks were increased until the competition tribunal intervened, and some well-known companies were fined.

8.13   Conclusion

The main aim of this chapter was to bring to the attention of family members some of the things that have an effect on their budgets, even if they may be unaware. The chapter presented the issues which have an impact on the finances of the middle class, low class and unemployed people as: demand and supply, imports and exports, rate of exchange, fuel price, interest rate, inflation, taxes, no fee schools and free higher education, infrastructure development and hosting of events, and corruption price fixing (collusion). Understanding these issues will help family members to contribute to ongoing narratives about these issues and have an influence on them. Also, family members can use their understanding of these issues for personal benefit and to avoid unnecessary loss.

BIBLIOGRAPHY

Msimanga, M.R. 2016. *Accounting for beginner learners.* Harrismith: Msimanga MR.